FUKUSHIMA

Also by William Sargent

The Well From Hell, 2011

Sea Level Rising, 2009

Just Seconds from the Ocean, 2008

Crab Wars, 2006

The House on Ipswich Marsh, 2005

Praise for Other Books:

"With his fine descriptions and lucid explanations, Sargent joins the company of Lewis Thomas and Stephen Jay Gould as a first-rate interpreter of modern science."
~ *Publisher's Weekly*

"It is a gem of Natural History... the best introduction to the original environment of the New England coast."
~ Dr. E. O. Wilson, Harvard University

"A joy to read."
~ *The Washington Post*

"A Great Read! Sargent takes us on a raucous jaunt through the New England forest, to see the big picture with unclouded eyes. A true biologist, he examines everything in sight and counts it relevant, connecting it with seamless prose into the rational new picture. It's a powerful boost to the new Nature religion that references us to Life on Earth."
~ Dr. Bernd Heinrich

It's science writing that reads like a novel, with all the page-turning excitement of a thriller."
~ William Martin

"Sargent can turn an event as mundane as a rising tide into poetry. This is a book for everyone who loves the shore, especially Cape Cod."
~ *The Boston Globe*

"If you only have time for one book about life-death dramas played to the sound of crashing waves, about new science and the old sea, about Nobel prizes, squid brains and sex orgies on Cape Cod beaches, then this book is for you."
~ Dr. A.A. Moscona, Journal of the
American Medical Association

FUKUSHIMA

BY

WILLIAM SARGENT

Published by 🍓 Strawberry Hill Press

Table Of Contents

Chapter One

Poised on The Ring of Fire
The Japanese Islands
750 Million years ago

The Japanese Islands sit on one of the most seismically active shards of geology on our planet. To understand their complicated history we must first review plate tectonics, the theory that changed our view of geology as thoroughly as the theory of evolution shaped our view of life on earth.

The surface of our planet is covered with 12 major plates and about 22 minor plates of the earth's crust. The plates carry both the older granitic continents that sit lightly on top and the younger, heavier basaltic slabs that make up the bottom of the oceans.

Slabs of this sea floor crust are constantly being created as they rise along a series of underwater volcanoes that encircle our globe like the seams on a baseball, and they are constantly being consumed as they are sucked back into the earth's interior at the plates' margins.

As the oceanic crust is pulled back toward the earth's molten interior it is warmed by the heat of the earth's radioactive decay. This creates magma that rises to the surface to create molten, often lava-belching volcanoes. This process is particularly apparent along the margins of the Pacific Ocean because that oceanic basin is both opening at the mid-oceanic ridge and being squeezed by the Atlantic oceanic basin that is opening faster on the other side of the globe. This battle between the Atlantic and Pacific Oceans and their tectonic forces of creation and destruction are what cause the many volcanoes that encircle the Pacific Ocean in what geologists call the "Ring of Fire."

Because the earth must always remain about the same size, the creation of crust at the center of the oceans is always matched by the consumption of crust at the margins. But, because the Atlantic Ocean is producing crust faster than the Pacific Ocean, the Pacific Ocean basin is gradually getting smaller and smaller and, if all goes according to plan, will close up entirely in a paroxysm of mountain building in 300 million years! With that as the briefest of introductions, let's look in more detail at the landmass we now call Japan.

Until about 750 million years ago, all the world's continents were clumped together into the supercontinent of Rodinia. But then, rifts above a rising plume of hot magma began breaking Rodinia apart. One of these rifts would become the Pacific Ocean. The seam of underwater volcanoes at the center of the Pacific also started creating a continuous slab of ocean floor that is still being carried west on the back of the earth's viscous mantle to the edge of Eurasian plate.

Then, about 300 million years ago, these same tectonic forces tore two small blocks of continental islands off of Rodinia, as it slowly continued to break apart. These cratons danced around each other for another few hundred million years until they finally were pushed into, and became part, of the Eurasian plate. There they became known as suspect terranes, which is just the fancy way geologists say, "We really don't know where the hell these rocks came from."

Moving ahead in time to about 15 million years ago, this conglomeration of eroded material and suspect terranes pulled away from the mainland, turned, and became lodged in its present location as an arc of volcanic islands called the Japanese

Archipelago. Today, this landmass sits rather uncomfortably between the tectonic forces moving the Pacific plate, the Eurasian plate and a broken off chip of the American plate called the Okhotsk micro plate.

And the process continues today. The same slab of ocean bottom creates the Japanese trench as it is sucked below the Eurasian plate, dragging coral reefs, seamounts and plateaus of planktonic oozes back into the earth's interior. Most of the lighter material is bulldozed into a wedge of accretionary material that makes up the eastern side of the islands, and the rest plunges below the Eurasian plate in a series of episodic jerks that we know as earthquakes. To date, almost 15,000 kilometers of ocean crust have plunged below the Japanese Islands during the past 450 million years. The resulting periodic earthquakes displace the ocean floor so dramatically that they create tsunamis that propagate back toward the Japanese coast as we saw so tragically March 11, 2011.

The Chrysanthemum and the Sword

It was these tectonic origins that shaped the political organization and character of Japan. A jagged range of high, young volcanic mountains run down the center of the archipelago like a spinal column. This makes most of the interior of Japan too steep for habitation, so small groups of people were forced to cluster around strong leaders, or daimyo, in the many small river valleys and flood plains that dot the East Coast of the islands. This led to a decentralized feudal system because each small coastal plain formed it's own autonomous political structure. For centuries the islands were made up of a collection of these small petty autonomous countries isolated by land, but accessible by water.

The swords of samurai warriors with traditional military codes of conduct and knightly honor protected these nascent states. Over time, the small feudal units became united under an emperor believed to be descended from the sun goddess, and whose family came to be represented by the flower of the red chrysanthemum. The chrysanthemum and the sword became the symbols that stood for both the military virtues of the samurai and fidelity to the nation as represented by the emperor. In 1946, the American cultural anthropologist Ruth Benedict wrote *The Chrysanthemum and the Sword*, a book that remains a bestseller in Japan and is still read in the United States today. The book was the first attempt by Americans to truly understand Japanese people after demonizing them during the Second World War. The term came to symbolize a respect for diversity that became one of the bedrock beliefs of liberalism during the Cold War in America. Today, it seems mostly to be remembered in reruns of "Mad Men", a popular comedy set in the benighted Fifties.

Japan's topography also shaped her agricultural practices. Unlike most northern latitude countries whose agriculture is limited by dry summers in the south and cool summers in the north, Japan is blessed with both hot summers and rain that falls bountifully from early spring to autumn. These attributes give Japan a long growing season; they also created an ideal situation for farmers to adapt the dry field rice cultivation practices imported from China into their own style of highly productive wet field rice paddy cultivation. Farmers maximize the growing season by working intensely all summer long, using 90 times more manpower per acre than their western counterparts.

Consequently, Japan has been able to grow two to four times more rice per acre than its counterparts in Southeast Asia.

This high productivity means that even though only 15 percent of Japan's landmass is suitable for agriculture, it has been able to support many more people per acre than countries in the Americas, Europe or West Asia, and it has been doing so for the past three centuries.

Among Japan's river valleys and coastal plains small clusters of people have developed effective processes to derive the most benefit from their small, shared water systems. It is interesting to note that after the Fukushima earthquake, one of the first things journalists noted was how even in the excluded nuclear zone, a family with extra water would put a note on their door inviting neighbors in to share the traditionally valuable commodity.

Despite its limited natural resources and having none of it's own sources of fossil fuel, Japan has been able to sustain the doubling of its population since the beginning of the 20th Century and attain one of the highest standards of living in the world.

Much of this has been achieved through massive industrialization, aided in large part by the building of more nuclear power plants per acre than any other nation on Earth. Until 2011, Japan was the second largest economy on Earth and the largest importer of oil, coal, iron, copper, cotton and wool.

There is another element of Japan's topography that has shaped its traditional worldview. Japan straddles the East Coast of Asia the way the East Coast of the United States straddles North America. Like the East Coast of the United States, whose climate is tempered by the Gulf Stream, the warm water Kurioshio or "black current" tempers Japan's climate. But there is a dark side to the black current. Like the Gulf Stream, the Kurioshio steers and strengthens the typhoons that are even more powerful than the hurricanes that plague the East Coast of America.

These typhoons have played a major role in Japanese history. One typhoon, the "kamikaze," or "divine wind," saved Japan by destroying the boats of her early Mongol invaders. But most typhoons are so frequent and dreaded that they have engendered a stoic fatalism, particularly among people that live along the highly populated East Coast. The characteristic is so pronounced that the Japanese call it a "typhoon mentality," which accepts nature's destructive power, but also is determined to dig out from such natural catastrophes and start all over again. This typhoon mentality had been tested again and again through wars, bombings, earthquakes and volcanoes. But it would be sorely tested by the earthquake, tsunami and nuclear tragedy that enveloped the country on March 11, 2011, when once again Japan would need to rely on the traditional powers of the chrysanthemum and the sword.

Chapter Two

Fact-Based Decision Making
The Geokids versus the Geosynclinists
The 1880s to the 1980s

From the late 1800s to the Cold War, geologists constructed a fairly shaky theory about how the earth was formed. According to this theory, radioactivity within the earth's core had gradually cooled, contracting our planet like a plum becoming a prune; only, the wrinkles on this prune became the mountain ranges that cover the earth today. Plains and valleys were formed as sea-level fluctuations covered and uncovered the continents, leaving behind a series of sediment-filled geosynclines and anticlines.

Scientists who adhered to this complicated theory came to be known as geosynclinists or, sometimes, fixed-earth proponents or simply, contractionists. Their opponents were called mobilists, because they clung to the equally eccentric theory that the continents could drift over the world's surface like so many battleships. Continental Drift had been propagated by the explorer and popular science writer Alfred Wegener who had looked at a globe and noticed, as have millions of school-aged children both before and since, that if you could move the African and American continents together they would fit together like pieces of a jigsaw puzzle. But the real puzzle was trying to figure how to move the continents in the first place.

This was where the state of theoretical geology sat for several generations, poised between two equally contrived and unsatisfying theories. But, for the most part, it didn't really matter. Geologists could still make significant discoveries outside of either theory. The Japanese seismologist Kiyoo Wadati made one such discovery. In 1928, Wadati observed that most of Japan's major earthquakes occurred parallel to oceanic trenches and deep within the earth along an area that sloped 40 to 60 degrees down toward the core of the planet. It turned out that the American seismologist Hugo Benioff was making similar observations on the other side of the world. Today, seismologists still refer to Wadati-Benioff zones, areas where powerful offshore earthquakes occur up to 420 miles below the earth's surface. That was where the research sat for several generations, a useful piece of knowledge that didn't seem to fit into either paradigm.

World War II injected huge amounts of cash into the study of seismology, because the allied navies wanted to know where German U-boats were lurking to avoid detection by sonar. Scientists from institutions like the Woods Hole Oceanographic Institution on the East Coast, and the Scripps Institute of Oceanography on the West Coast were sent out to explore the ocean floor.

Their methods were simple; they just threw sticks of dynamite overboard and measured how long it took echoes from the explosions to return to their recording devices. One of the ships was the beautiful sailing vessel Atlantis, owned by the Woods Hole Oceanographic Institution. Seismologists aboard the ship liked to call themselves WHOI scientists after the acronym for the esteemed institution. But it came out sounding more like "Hooey scientists," to the annoyance of the institution's administrators who were trying to broadcast a more polished image to the world community.

However, each cruise brought back new revelations. Researchers discovered, first, that the bottom of the Atlantic Ocean was not just a huge featureless plain of accumulated sediments. Instead, it had guyots or seamounts and underwater volcanoes that formed a ragged range of mountains they called the Mid-Atlantic Ridge. Later, they discovered that the Mid-Atlantic Ridge was just a short piece of a 50,000-kilometer-long range of underwater volcanoes that girdle the globe like the seams on a baseball. Although this mid-oceanic ridge system is largely invisible because it lies below the ocean, it is our planet's largest geological feature.

Then, in 1947, WHOI scientists made recordings of returning sonar echoes that showed layers of sediment on the ocean floor that were much thinner than scientists thought they should be. This was a quandary. Geologists knew that the world was about four billion years old based on the rate of decay the earth's radioactive core, so there should be about five kilometers worth of sediment lying on the ocean floor. Instead, researchers found only a few kilometers worth of sediment. This was very strange, but it was matched by an even more curious observation.

During World War II the US Navy had used airborne magnetometers to detect the metal hulls of submarines. After the war these magnetometers were modified so they could be towed behind ships to study the sea floor. Oceanographers started seeing odd symmetrical patterns in the magnetic signatures of the earth's crust on either side of mid-oceanic ridges. They discovered that the earth's crust is composed of basalt that is molten when it emerges, and as it cools, tiny grains of magnetite line up in accordance to the earth's magnetic field. But in one strip of basalt, all the grains of magnetite were pointing toward the North Pole and in the adjoining strip of basalt, all the grains of magnetite were pointing toward the South Pole.

Another Japanese scientist, Motonari Matuyama, had discovered the same magnetic variations in the 1920s and decided it meant that the earth's magnetic field must have reversed in the past. Now we know the earth's magnetic field flips about every million years or so.

All of a sudden these tiny bits of information started to make Alfred Wegner's long ridiculed theory of continental drift make some sense after all. Perhaps molten ocean crust was rising up out of the world's interior along the mid-oceanic ridge systems and pushing the continents apart. But there was one problem. If the earth was creating all of this new material why wasn't our planet growing larger and larger?

The American geologist Harry Hess realized that Kiyoo Wadati had discovered the reason 40 years before. It was in the Wadati-Benieff zones that the new crust was being recycled back into the earth's interior. In 1962 Hess presented a paper at Cambridge University; by all accounts it was a bravura presentation. He used his new concept of sea floor spreading to explain the location of earthquakes, volcanoes, deep trenches, valuable mineral resources, and the Pacific's ominous Ring of Fire. But he called his paper Geopoetry because he felt scientists still didn't have enough hard data to thoroughly back up his musings.

But the die had been cast. Throughout the Sixties oceanographers started to collect that hard data, and today we have the theory, satisfying at last, of plate tectonics.

However, paradigms shift in mysterious ways. Everyone doesn't always see the light at exactly the same time. One wag has said that paradigms shift more through retirements and funerals than by academics actually changing their minds.

I remember taking an undergraduate 'gut' course called "Rocks for Jocks." It was in 1968 and Harvard's geology department was split down the middle between the older professors who still used the complicated system of geosynclines and anticlines, and the younger professors who had already adopted plate tectonics.

So, the course was presented as a debate between the two sides. Even as callow undergraduates we understood we were witnessing an intellectual revolution and could see that plate tectonics was clearly the better way of understanding the world.

Japan went through a similar debate between the older professors whom they called the Geosynclinists and the younger professors they called the Geokids. It would have remained as just another one of those quaint but unimportant little ivory tower disputes if Japan had not been deciding where to place about 55 nuclear reactors in order to meet its insatiable demand for energy.

However, while the United States had resolved its plate tectonics debate in the 1970s, Japan did not resolve its debate until the late 1980s. But Japan built most of its nuclear reactors in the 1970s when the geosynclinists still headed most of the university geology departments and decided which professors to hire. If the decisions about whether to adopt nuclear energy and where to place nuclear reactors had been made by the Geokids in the 1980s instead of the Geosynclinists in the 1970s, it is unlikely Japan would have built 55 nuclear reactors on one the most seismically active spots on our planet.

A similar situation happened in the Soviet Union in the 1940s when an unschooled former peasant called Trofim Lysenko convinced Joseph Stalin and later Nikita Khrushchev that evolution and genetics were just bourgeoisie western pseudo sciences and that if crops could only be grown along good communist principles then harvests would be quadrupled. He had geneticists exiled to political prisons; consequently, agriculture stagnated in the Soviet Union from the 1940s to when Lysenko was finally ousted in 1964.

The United States has gone through similar situations. But instead of scientists debating amongst themselves, it has often been right-wing pundits like Glenn Beck and Rush Limbaugh who have argued against evolution and debunked global warming as the greatest hoax ever pulled on the American people.

Of course, the truth will eventually will out, but at what cost? Will decisions like prohibiting the EPA from regulating greenhouse gases look as foolhardy to our grandchildren as building 55 nuclear reactors look to most Japanese citizens today? I fear they will.

Chapter Three

"Climb the Mountain!"
March 11, 2011
2:46 PM

For several months the weight of the Pacific plate had been pulling down the Okhotsk plate beneath the island of Honshu. This was causing stress to build in the upper plate that wanted to spring back toward the surface. On March 9, the Okhotsk plate did lurch upward; three more earthquakes followed over magnitude 6.

These quakes were bad enough, but on March 11, at 2:46 p.m., just when most workers were taking a Ramen break and parents were preparing to pick up their children from school, about 300 miles of the Okhotsk plate snapped upward, moving the island of Honshu eight feet closer to America and causing 250 miles of the coastline of Japan to drop two feet. This would allow the ensuing tsunami to travel further and faster inland. The magnitude 9 earthquake lasted for six minutes, releasing enough energy to power the city of Los Angeles for an entire year, or in Japanese terms, 600 million times more energy than released by the bomb that flattened Hiroshima. Two days after the quake, the Shinmoedake volcano erupted on the island of Kyushu and in Antarctica the Williams glacier slipped two feet closer to the ocean. The earth started rotating almost a second faster.

Signals from Japan's system of a thousand seismometers arrived in Tokyo a minute before the quake, giving millions of people scant warning but possibly just enough time to have saved thousands of lives. At first people thought it was just another earthquake. Everyone knew the drill. Younger office workers pulled out their cells and tweeted, "Felt that one," or "Ground shaking," to all their nearest and dearest friends.

But this was something different; people became nauseous with motion sickness as their buildings started to sway. Asphalt on the highways heaved up and down making cars hop into the air like toys being shaken off a rug. Workers in skyscrapers snapped pictures of computers sliding off their desks, but trusted that the spongy hydraulic platforms beneath their buildings would keep the 30 story behemoths from collapsing into so many heaps of rubble.

As the quake continued, young people's tweets started to take on a more ominous tone, "This is the largest and most frightening quake I have ever encountered." Older office workers crowded into the reinforced disaster prevention rooms, but the shaking continued—one, two, three, four, five, six minutes. Even after the quake stopped people continued to sway back and forth to compensate for the former rolling. But, the only way to really tell if the earthquake had stopped was to look at a ceiling lamp and see if it was still swaying.

Someone near the window of the Avnet office yelled that there was black smoke pouring out of a high rise building in Obaiba. The ground had liquefied beneath the manmade island in Tokyo Harbor. Bob Hackett remembered thinking that the aftershocks that occurred a few minutes after the quake were the second largest earthquakes he had ever experienced.

The elevators had automatically shut down in all the skyscrapers, so long lines of office workers slowly started to climb down the poorly lit stairwells. Wives texted their whereabouts to their husbands and mothers took whatever transportation they could find to pick up their kids at school.

Thousands of people dressed in dark suits and high heels trudged patiently down the trafficless streets of Tokyo. The train stations were closed and eerily silent. Everyone was determined to get back to their loved ones before nightfall and the threat of more aftershocks in the dark. Thousands of people slept in their cars that night.

It had been a day of a thousand acts of courage, kindness and determination. People had urged each other on with the term "gambaro," stay strong and stand firm, and "gamen," to be quietly enduring. This was Japan's typhoon mentality kicking in—she would pull herself together and rebuild. It was a testament to the skill of Japan's engineers that so few people had died in their earthquake-proof skyscrapers. But there was a problem. Who would want to return to a 30-story-tall skyscraper during the coming months of aftershocks? It was only when Tokyoites returned home and turned on their television sets that they learned the true horror of what their country had just endured.

The Tsunamis

Immediately after the earthquake struck, the Japan Meteorological Agency started issuing warnings for a major tsunami, the highest rating on their scale of woe. They predicted that the tsunamis would top 30 feet and start arriving within 10 to 30 minutes of the earthquake. They warned that people should immediately evacuate the coasts and repair to higher ground. The first tsunamis started arriving 30 minutes after the quake and were over three stories high in the fishing port of Onagana, home to the Onagana nuclear power plant, which was shut down because of fires in its turbine room. Like the 2004 Indian Ocean earthquake, the tsunami was far more deadly that the actual quake, heavily damaging or totally destroying 16 cites and covering a total area of over 300 square miles.

Thousands of husbands were trapped in skyscrapers in Tokyo, frantically trying to reach their wives and children living in the coastal communities threatened by the tsunamis.

Edam Corkill was in his office in Tokyo, trying to concentrate on his work while also monitoring the tsunamis on television. He remembered that when he first moved his family to Zushi City he had looked at a tsunami hazard map. It only showed their home being lightly grazed by a few centimeters of water. He figured it would only be like a small wave rushing up the beach and soaking your towel. The old timers said they would stay in Zushi City during a tsunami because one had never occurred in their lifetimes. Edam wondered how many families with children had listened to the old men.

The NKT radio station was reporting in its no nonsense way that the tsunami was expected to arrive on the Miura Peninsula in 45 minutes. Edam emailed his wife, "Climb the Mountain! Climb the mountain! Escape! Escape!" … No answer.

He watched as the warnings changed from orange, "tsunami," to red, "major tsunami." He e-mailed again, "Climb the Mountain! Take the emergency radio! Listen to it! CLIMB THE MOUNTAIN NOW!!"

Edam watched as the tsunamis inundated the Sendai airport. They were not blue like the Indian Ocean tsunamis, but black and muddy and they continued to sweep through the city, not receding like a wave, but advancing like an incoming tide that would never stop. Boats, cars, busses and houses rolled over and over in their wake.

He turned away and started getting ready to sleep in his cubicle as the building continued to shake and rattle. He felt sick to his stomach and wondered how he and many other men had convinced their wives to rent homes by the sea so they could surf, sail and fish on the weekends. How many other men felt guilty for endangering the life of their wives and children?

At 6:40 Edam sent a jubilant email to his father, "Keiko climbed the mountain. Now she is in the public library. No major tsunami has yet hit Zushi City."

A teacher in Canada was watching the news before heading off to school. A reporter was with a 10-year-old boy and his grandfather and aunt looking for his mother. As the young boy searched through the wreckage of his former home, his grandfather yelled. He had found the family car pushed up against their home. He could see his daughter's small white face still strapped inside.

The boy's aunt rushed to the car and slapped her hands on the windshield. The boy beamed, thinking his nightmare would soon be over. No more police, no more sirens, no more ambulances. They had found his mother and he would soon have her safe and sound at home. He didn't realize that his aunt was keening with grief. The teacher switched off the set. How would he face his class of 10-year-olds so eager to face their bright futures safe in Canada?

By the end of the week, one person wrote that the most difficult thing to accept was that Japan was in a war zone but it had no human enemy to blame. They had just been pummeled by an implacable force of nature that didn't care whether they lived or died. Other people wrote that the recent rash of volcanoes, earthquakes, tsunamis and hurricanes was the work of God and meant that the earth was coming to an end.

In fact, these disasters indicate that we exist on a living, breathing growing planet. Although our world is almost five billion years old, it is a mere adolescent in planetary terms. The seismic events we experience as personal affronts are merely the hormonal rages of an adolescent planet that doesn't care if we exist or not.

If the volcanoes, earthquakes and tsunamis were to suddenly die out and our planet turned cool and stable, it would be the signal that we were living on a dying planet. Despite the danger and drama of living on our restless earth, most of us would probably prefer to live on a young, living, breathing planet than on an old crone of a planet slumping slowly toward her grave on the edge of an abyss of cold, black entropy.

Chapter Four

"San Ten Ichi Ichi"
Fukushima
March 11, 2011
"Station Blackout"

Immediately after the Fukushima earthquake, the world breathed a sigh of relief. Japanese engineering had saved the day. There had been far fewer deaths than expected, and tsunamis had not crossed the Pacific causing hundreds of thousands more deaths as they had done after the Indonesian earthquake in 2004.

The world didn't expect to see a massive explosion at the Fukushima nuclear power plant the day after the earthquake. Uncertainty reigned. Was this the beginning of the famed "China syndrome," where nuclear fuel melts down through the earth to come out in China? Of course in China, they probably call this the "Boston Syndrome."

But what the public didn't realize is that the problem had started when the earthquake had first jolted Fukushima Daichi, or Fukushima One. Kazuma Yokato was already at Fukushima Daichi for a routine inspection. After crawling out from under his desk the young inspector for Japan's Nuclear Industrial and Safety Agency surveyed the situation.

Everything appeared to have worked as designed. The system had automatically shut down reactors one, two and three. Reactors four and five were already shut down for maintenance.

Tepco, the Tokyo Electric Power Company, had been upgrading the facility so they could obtain permission to extend its life.

Yokato didn't realize that the quake had knocked out an electric transfer station six miles from the plant. This meant that the plant wouldn't be able to obtain electricity off the national grid. Instead, they would have to rely on 13 diesel generators to provide electricity to the pumps that circulated water over the radioactive fuel rods. Each generator was the size of a locomotive. When all the generators were in operation you couldn't hear yourself think. But at the moment it was the sound that Yokato desperately wanted to continue hearing.

3:01

Yokato was walking toward the emergency evacuation post at the west gate when the first tsunami crashed over the mile long breakwater and 17-foot-high sea wall built to protect the plant. It was 3:01 pm, only 15 minutes after the quake.

The 45-foot wave inundated the building, which sat only 30 feet above sea level. When the wave receded the damage was plain to see. Salt water had shorted out the electrical circuitry of 12 of the 13 generators. Tepco informed the government it had experienced "station blackout." Now the fate of the plant rested on batteries designed to provide only 12 hours of extra power. The engineers called them "coping batteries," because they only gave you 12 hours to solve all your problems.

It was only when Yokato drove to Okuma that he realized things were even worse than he had expected. Tepco's command office was in shambles and communications were down. He wouldn't be able to contact anyone from the damaged office, so he returned to the earthquake-proof bunker at Fukushima.

The white bunker had thick concrete walls and a special filtration system to protect against radiation. It would be his home for the next few days. He joined Masao Yoshida who had set up the center only the day before. Yoshida knew the inside of Fukushima Daichi like the back of his hand. He was Vice Chairman of the group set up to study how to extend the life of the aging facility. But he was also not afraid to deliver bad news, and the bad news was about to get even worse.

A nuclear reactor is like a giant kettle; as long as water continues to circulate over the fuel rods in the containment vessel, the water will keep them cool enough to operate safely. However, if the water stops flowing, the fuel rods will start to boil away the water, and be exposed to the air. This will cause the rods to burst into flames, releasing radioactive gases into the atmosphere. It is the beginning of a nuclear meltdown.

However, the Tepco engineers couldn't tell if they were experiencing a meltdown, because the meters designed to measure the flow of water had also been damaged, and they couldn't tell if the coping batteries were still working.

But they knew something was wrong. At 7:30 p.m. Prime Minister Kan declared the situation a nuclear emergency and created a three-kilometer evacuation. It would be expanded to 20 kilometers less than 24 hours later. People started referring to the disaster as "san ten ichi ichi," March 11, 2011.

The Hydrogen Explosion
March 12, 2011

By the second day of the crisis, the coping batteries had quite definitely gone dead. Water in the first reactor was so low that more than five feet of fuel rods were exposed, and radioactive steam and hydrogen from the breakdown of water were building up rapidly in the reactor. It was the first time active fuel rods had been exposed to the atmosphere in the 30-year history of the plant.

Tepco started to vent off the highly flammable hydrogen. It was the lesser of two evils, but it was also too little too late. At 3:30 in the afternoon of March 12th, a massive hydrogen explosion ripped through the outer structure of Fukushima Daichi, blowing out the concrete walls and causing the radiation levels to spike. The explosion injured four workers and was followed by two more hydrogen explosions during the following 62 hours.

The government spokesman announced that the concrete building had collapsed but the reactor itself had not been damaged. It seemed like a distinction without a difference when the evacuation zone was increased again to 20 kilometers—almost six miles.

But the explosions were not the worst of the multiplying problems facing workers inside the buildings. Each reactor contained a 40-foot-deep lighted pool that emitted an eerie blue color. These were the spent fuel pools that also had to be constantly covered with water to prevent the spent rods from overheating. Evidently, the initial quake had opened a crack in one of the pools. But by now, the engineers had run out of options for repairing it.

Radioactive Fire
March 15

On March 15, a fire broke out around the 1,300 spent fuel rods stored on top of reactor four. Engineers around the world suddenly realized that they had entered new territory. In the words of Edward Morse, professor of nuclear engineering at University of California in Berkley, "That turned out to be the most terrifying event throughout the whole ordeal. They had no containment structure whatsoever. They didn't even have a roof."

Now Tepco had to deal with three potential meltdowns, a fire spewing radioactive gases into the atmosphere and three reactors continuing to fill with explosive hydrogen gas. Plus, the fire was preventing workers from gaining access to the building to try to gain some control over of the situation.

Was Tepco facing the possibility of three China Syndrome meltdowns occurring in the same plant, simultaneously? The engineers couldn't tell. This situation was far more complicated than anything anyone had ever faced at Three Mile Island or Chernobyl. It was also a pretty good reminder that you probably didn't want to build six reactors on a single site.

Tepco decided to throw everything it could find into the mix. It leased fire engines, helicopters and special trucks that could either spray tons of water out of special crowd control cannons or turn around and pour concrete out of a 90-foot boom to encase the reactors. The world witnessed the sight of helicopters ineffectually trying to drop buckets of water onto the reactors while staying out of clouds of smoke and nuclear particles rising from the stricken plant. It was not a reassuring sight.

But the fire in the spent fuel pools was the most immediately worrisome problem. Because the fuel was still fresh it had large volumes of iodine and cesium that could be carried at least 20 kilometers from the site and remain radioactive for up to 10,000 years.

The public quickly became familiar with how radiation was measured. On two occasions, radiation levels within the plant had reached one sievert an hour. Thirty minutes of exposure to that dose would trigger nausea; four hours of exposure at that level would lead to death within four months. The danger to the 50 anonymous workers who had been revolving in and out of the plant became readily apparent and they became international heroes.

March 31

As the first month of the crisis came to a close, electricity had finally been restored and the reactors had cooled down a bit because salt water was being pumped through the reactors. But the salt water would eventually create it's own problems because of its corrosive nature. Radioactive levels were recorded to be 1,000 millisieverts, enough to kill anyone exposed for short amounts of time.

Rescue workers had also found the bodies of two workers who had either been crushed during the initial earthquake or been drowned by the resultant tsunami. The discovery was a stark reminder that problems were still being uncovered and still cascading through the system. To make matters worse, powerful aftershocks continued to plague the area, reversing progress that was made only days before. But, despite conflicting reports, things were very slowly starting to improve.

Chapter Five

Where It All Began
Nuclear Subs
1954

When President Obama introduced his 2010 energy bill, it included funding for research on a new generation of small, mobile nuclear power plants that could be hooked up to existing energy facilities to help cut down the emission of greenhouse gases. The idea behind the funding was that if an accident did occur in these plants, damage would be limited, because of their small size. To bolster this argument, Obama cited the U.S. Navy's long history of safely building compact nuclear reactors to power its atomic submarines.

The military often has the vision and wherewithal to capitalize on new forms of energy faster than the private sector. In 1915, Winston Churchill convinced the Admiralty to switch its warships from burning coal to burning oil. As part of the deal, he helped the Anglo-Persian oil company obtain a monopoly on Persian oil. The nationalized company eventually became what we now call BP. Many historians claim that both World War I and World War II were won on this flood of oil, first from Iran and later from America.

The first person to propose nuclear submarines was Ross Gunn from the Office of Naval Research. The deputy chief of naval operations, Admiral Carney, opposed the idea. Carney urged that the world ban nuclear powered warships altogether, fearing that if America built such a fleet her enemies would surely follow suit, as they surely did.

But the military advantages of nuclear submarines were just too obvious to ignore. Nuclear submarines could cruise silently for months at a time without having to resurface for fuel. The major disadvantage turned out to be that nuclear power plants produced so much heat and radioactivity that they trailed telltale wakes of hot water that could be detected by satellites.

The true father of the American submarine fleet was Admiral Hyman Rickover. In 1951, he convinced Congress to put up $55 million to build the world's first nuclear submarine. It is a testament to Admiral Rickover's powers of persuasion, and the Navy's clout, that the U.S.S. Nautilus was completed in less than four years. Today, it would take a private company at least 12 years just to get the permits to build a nuclear facility, if they could get permission at all.

The U.S.S. Nautilus proved to be so successful that both the U.S. and the Soviet Union continued to churn out nuclear submarines. Today, the oceans are full nuclear powered submarines, the most advanced packing warheads capable of incinerating 200 cities at a time, from 4,500 miles away. They are being operated successfully by the U.S., Russia, Great Britain, France, China and India.

The principle behind a submarine's nuclear power plant is the same as that behind the reactors at the Fukushima facility. The reactors contain highly enriched fuel rods in shielded containment vessels that can provide energy continuously for up to 30 years. The rods make steam to power turbines. The turbines can either turn the propellers directly or power electric motors to run the boat.

Like the Fukushima plants, the submarines also have diesel

generators to provide back-up power if the reactors fail. The primary requirement of the plants is that they be compact enough to fit into a submarine and safe enough for sailors to be able to live beside them for years at a time. The reactors are about a 20th the size of most commercial plants and have been reliably described as finely tuned as a 4,000-ton, underwater, Swiss watch. As the Navy likes to say, "We build our reactors safely because we have to sleep beside them."

But it is difficult to ascertain the military's actual record because most of the information about nuclear safety is so highly nuanced. The U.S. and Russia both tend to characterize their own mishaps as "incidents," but those of their enemies as "accidents," if not "full-blown catastrophes." This has allowed Admiral Rickover to repeat the oft-quoted mantra that the U.S. Navy has never had a nuclear accident, despite having at least two "incidents," where submarines sank with the loss of their entire crews. However, by reading between the lines of the U.S. reports about Soviet accidents and the Soviet reports about U.S. accidents you can get a fairly accurate picture.

Overall, the military's safety record does appear to be much better than that of privately-owned, land-based reactors. There have been accidents; in fact, more than on land-based facilities. As far as we know, however, the accidents have been relatively benign from a nuclear point of view though catastrophic to the hundreds of sailors on the sunken submarines. But because subs sink, far less actual fallout is released into the atmosphere than would occur in an accident at a land-based facility. Plus, the same lead shielding that is designed to protect the sailors is also designed to prevent radiation from leaking into the marine environment if an accident does occur. There have been three nuclear accidents where an uncontrolled chain reaction led to a partial meltdown; there have been approximately seven loss-of-coolant accidents. Most of these occurred while the submarines were being built or were in port for repairs. Three of the coolant-loss accidents occurred when reactors automatically ignited as control rods were raised into a higher position. Some of the accidents actually occurred when Soviets and Americans were playing ridiculously dangerous games of underwater chicken.

In 1985 at the Vladivostock shipyard a Soviet Victor class reactor exploded, contaminating a six-kilometer area on the Shotovo Peninsula and marine waters outside of the plant. Ten people were killed in the accident; the damaged reactor still contains its nuclear fuel. It is a well-known fact that within many Russian homes are retired sailors who lost their hair because of radiation exposure while serving aboard Soviet submarines.

At least six Soviet submarines and three American nuclear subs, The U.S.S. Thresher, the U.S.S. Scorpion and the U.S.S. Seawolf, now lie on the ocean floor as a result of accidents or collisions. At least one Soviet sub was scuttled in the Kara Sea when Russian officials decided it would be cheaper to sink the vessel than to decommission its reactor.

As far as we know, the shutdown mechanisms on all the sunken submarines have been fully engaged to prevent radiation from getting into the marine environment. In some cases sailors lost their lives to radiation sickness after having to manually lower the fuel rods before the submarine sank. In others the automatic system had kicked in as it should. However, nobody has been funded to do the research to know exactly how much radiation has entered the marine food chain from these mishaps.

In many ways the use of nuclear technology in submarines is similar to the use of sophisticated technology in space exploration. Both have to contend with unforgiving environments, whether it be zero gravity in space or hull-crushing pressure in the deep ocean.

Considering the number of submariners who have had to live beside nuclear reactors for so long, the number of exposure-related deaths has been relatively low. The damage to the environment remains largely unknown, a mixed record at best and one that should give us some pause.

In a world where global warming is having an increasing impact on our lives, small, mobile, nuclear power plants, similar to those on nuclear submarines might still have a role to play in reducing greenhouse gas emissions. But the danger we face with any fuel is that we become inured to its downsides. When an oil spill occurs it is simply too easy to say, "Well that was too bad but we needed the oil," or when a nuclear accident occurs and hundreds of thousands of people have to leave their homes never to return, it is simply too easy to say, "Well that was too bad, but we needed that nuclear energy." Eventually, we will have to decide if some fuels are simply too risky to continue using.

Chapter Six

Three Mile Island and Chernobyl

The Three Mile Island nuclear power plant sits appropriately on Three Mile Island in the Susquehanna River, 10 miles north of Harrisburg, Pennsylvania. In 1979, it was using water pumped from the river to cool its two twin reactors.

But at 4 a.m. on March 28 of that year, the small inlet valve on the second reactor failed, causing temperatures to rise inside the unit. This triggered the plant's computerized safety system to raise the reactor's control rods so the nuclear chain reaction would stop. The automatic procedure solved the immediate problem, but the reactor's core temperature continued to climb due to residual heat in the fuel rods.

At this point, less than a minute into the emergency, a second automatic cooling system kicked in and started to divert extra water into the reactor core to cool it down. But the human operator on duty thought that water was still flowing normally through the failed valve so he aborted the emergency system. This caused steam to build up inside the reactor which then triggered a third emergency system to automatically open a safety valve on the top of the reactor, which released some slightly radioactive steam.

The maneuver should have cooled down the reactor but the new safety valve also jammed, allowing so much steam to escape that not enough water was left to cool the core. The human operator didn't know he had a problem because the valve's indicator light was hidden behind a recently-installed maintenance tag. And anyway, the core temperature had stopped rising so the problem wasn't readily apparent. He still didn't know that the pump outlets were closed, so when the emergency cooling system started pumping in extra water he shut it down again.

At this point the fuel rods started to collapse, letting the operator knew he had a critical problem. But, he still didn't know what was causing the problem. Only five minutes had elapsed since the initial valve had failed, and he had already made three major but understandable mistakes based on faulty information.

When the morning shift reported to work, they discovered that the steam valve on top of the reactor was open and closed it down. But it was already too late. Hydrogen gas had built up to explosive levels inside the core and the fuel rods were already melting in the containment vessel. This was what is called a partial meltdown. By late afternoon, there was a massive explosion of hydrogen gas, which destroyed most of the building containing the reactor but apparently not harming the critical fuel-rod containment vessel. This would have made it a complete meltdown.

Two weeks later, most of the hydrogen had dissolved back into the coolant water and the unit was brought back to a cold shutdown. The accident was over. Nobody had been injured. But radiation had been released into the atmosphere and into the Susquehanna River, which was the main source of the drinking water for downtown Harrisburg. To this day, nobody really knows what the effects of these releases will be on the people living around the plant or drinking water from the Susquehanna.

Chernobyl

The Chernobyl nuclear power plant is located about 80 miles north of Kiev in the present-day state of Ukraine. On April 26, 1986 the human operators of the Soviet plant were preparing to perform an experiment to see if residual energy from the plant's turbines could provide enough power to pump river water into the plant in the event of a power grid failure. The turbines would only have to do the job for a minute until the backup diesel generators could take over. It was a scenario similar to that faced by the operators of the Fukushima plant after the 2011 tsunami destroyed their connection to the power grid.

The Soviet operators needed to lower the plant's output prior to the test, but for some reason the power dropped to almost zero so the operators removed the reactor control rods to reinvigorate the chain reaction. The procedure appeared to work and the power output returned to normal.

The operators also turned on two pumps to increase the amount of water flowing out of the reactor. This cooled the reactor, but it also reduced the amount of water in the steam separator, so when the operators increased the flow of water and removed more control rods, the increased heat caused the coolant water to boil and form steam, which could potentially build up and cause an explosion.

As the test began the operator retracted more control rods to increase reactivity in the core, which was against the usual protocol. Under normal operating procedures 15 control rods were always supposed to remain in place, but because this was a test, the engineers had allowed themselves to go down to 10 rods. But the on-duty operator didn't realize how much steam had already built up in the reactor. As soon as he recognized his mistake he bolted from the reactor, but it was too late. The fuel rods had already started to shatter, which caused two explosions, breaking the containment vessel and blowing the roof off the reactor, which spewed radioactivity into the atmosphere.

Soviet officials tried to cover up the accident as nuclear particles fell on the citizens of major population centers throughout the Soviet Union and Northern Europe. Hundreds of people were exposed as they worked frantically to quell the radioactive fire. The world and Soviet citizens only heard about the accident when the fallout triggered monitors at a nuclear plant in Sweden.

The amount of radiation released from the accident was 200 times more than that of the Hiroshima and Nagasaki bombs, combined. Levels in Scotland were 10,000 times higher than normal. Thirty people died as a direct result of fighting the fire after the accident, and the rate of thyroid cancer in the Ukraine is still 20 times higher than before the accident.

Eventually, the Soviet government dumped over 300,000 metric tons of concrete over the reactor in an effort to entomb it, in what was described as an impregnable sarcophagus. But 10 years after the accident, holes had already started to appear in the top of the sarcophagus, which were allowing corrosive rainwater to seep inside. Engineers are still trying to find ways to replace the jerry-rigged structure.

It was the first major accident where a containment vessel had been breached. Both the accidents had started with mechanical failures that left the operators in the dark, frantically trying to make adjustments to the many problems cascading down on them. Their terror and frustration only increased the danger. The experiences of the operators would have a familiar ring when officials started to sort through the evidence to discover exactly what had gone wrong at Fukushima.

Chapter Seven

The Silver Lining

"We have the chance of becoming the first, big industrial nation to make the switch to renewable energy."

Angela Markel
May 31, 2011

At 4 a.m., only 14 hours after the Fukushima quake, Masao Yoshida was not only sleep deprived and terrified, he was mad as hell at Sakae Muto, Vice President of the Tokyo Electric Power Company. Pressure inside Fukushima Daichi's Unit One reactor had already gone to twice what the unit was designed for. Government officials were so rattled they ordered Tepco to begin venting hydrogen gas immediately.

Yoshida agreed. As director of the facility he also felt it was imperative to start venting to avoid a complete "China Syndrome" meltdown.

But Muto was afraid of the negative publicity. An unnamed government official was quoted as saying, "The two engaged in a heated shouting match—a rarity in reserved Japan. There was hesitation, arguments and sheer confusion."

A full 17 hours after the tsunami, and six hours after the government ordered them to do so, Tepco finally started venting, but the operators encountered a series of cascading problems eerily similar to what had happened at both Three Mile Island

and Chernobyl.

Fukushima's venting system was designed by General Electric to be operated from the control room, but because the power grid was down, that was not an option. Yoshida instead ordered several workers to enter the reactor and manually vent the system. However, radiation levels were so high that the exposed workers could not even reach the stricken reactor in Unit One.

In Unit Two, workers were able to open the safety valves inside the venting system, but for some reason the reactor pressure did not fall. In the number Three reactor, workers the safety valves closed every time they were manually opened.

The results were disastrous. Reactor One exploded the day after the quake, followed by Reactor Two days later and Reactor Three the day after that.

Each explosion sent several thousand times more radioactivity into the atmosphere than if the hydrogen had been vented when Yoshida first wanted it to be done. Within days, radioactive isotopes were being detected in drinking water as far away as California and Massachusetts.

It was only in May, two months after the earthquake, that Tepco started to admit that damage from the delay had been much worse than they had initially told either the government or the public. The fuel rods in all three reactors had completely melted, and the containment vessel in Reactor One had most likely ruptured, leading to massive contamination of both land and ocean scores of miles from the stricken reactor. Over 100,000 people had been permanently evacuated from the exclusionary red zone, and the ocean area around the site had been indefinitely closed to fishing.

Muto tried to have Yoshida fired for insubordination because he had also refused to stop pumping seawater into the stricken reactors. But the vice president was overruled by the other blue suits in the company. Yoshida was the only person capable of bringing the plant to a cold shutdown by Tepco's optimistic deadline of nine months, more than a year after the accident had occurred.

The Silver Lining

On the last day of May Angela Merkel announced that because of Fukushima, Germany would close down all of it's 17 nuclear power plants within 11 years, and double its use of renewable energy. This jolted the business world even more than the earthquake had rocked the planet. Switzerland and Italy had already signaled that they would cut back on their reliance on nuclear energy and China, which accounted for 44 percent of the all the nuclear power plants under construction, announced it would suspend approvals for any new nuclear plant until new safety regulations could be promulgated. But Germany was Europe's largest economy and the first major industrial nation to announce it would double its use of renewable energy.

The response was predictable: nuclear stocks plummeted and investments in solar panels and wind turbines soared. In the long term, this investment and increased demand would drastically reduce the cost of renewables. But the biggest short-term winner was the natural gas industry. Natural gas is cleaner than both coal and oil and is relatively abundant in Europe, the Middle East and Azerbaijan, which could be linked to Europe by pipeline as soon as 2017.

So perhaps there is a silver lining to the Fukushima accident. It has finally forced humans to face our two biggest environmental problems: global warming and dwindling oil resources.

Almost all the major social and political events of the past few decades, whether they be wars, unrest in the Middle East, Fukushima or the BP spill, have ultimately all revolved around these two interlocking problems.

It is also interesting how the public perception of Fukushima evolved as compared to that around the BP oil spill. When the world first learned about the BP spill it was regarded as the worst environmental accident of the century. It certainly looked like it. Thousands of tons of oil were spewing out of the seabed everyday. But when scientists finally started tallying up the data they realized the world had actually dodged a bullet; the spill had not permanently destroyed the Gulf of Mexico's major fisheries. In fact, the catch of many of the fisheries had improved because the fish had been able to grow and reproduce during the many months when the Gulf was closed to fishing.

Almost the opposite thing happened with Fukushima. Initial reports said it was a minor accident, less than what happened at Three Mile Island and Chernobyl. A little more than a week after the earthquake, NATO forces started bombing Libya and all the major news outlets had switched their operations from Japan to the Middle East. It was like the Fukushima crisis was over; time for the next big thing.

Of course, the crisis was far from over. It was only in May, two months after the accident, that international scientists were able to visit the site and evaluate what had actually happened. When they did, they began to realize that damage to the reactors and the environment had been far worse than what the public had been initially told.

Japan had suffered three complete meltdowns, and over 100,000 tons of water would have to be decontaminated. Plus, the reactors still had to cooled to below the boiling point of water, which could take as much as a year. The accident was upgraded to Level 7, the same as Chernobyl. The world had just witnessed its worst nuclear and environmental disaster in history and, like Chernobyl, the information had been buried to avoid public criticism.

The media had moved on to the love children of Arnold Schwarzenegger and John Edwards, and the tweets of Representative Weiner's bulging crotch. Perhaps that is to be expected. Our species only seems to be able to concentrate on inconvenient truths for so long, before our focus shifts back to ourselves and the lives and foibles of our extended families and celebrities.

William Sargent is a consultant for the NOVA Science series and the author of over a dozen books on science and the environment. His latest book, *The Well From Hell; The BP Spill and the Endurance of Big Oil* is available at local bookstores and through http://www.strawberryhillpress.com.